MW01089369

Seniors on the

Extending Your Life One Step at a Time

Introductory Comments

Seniors is not a group that is usually associated with running. By the time most seniors get there AARP Membership invitation at age 50, the last thing on their mind is to be out running. Images of falling, twisting an ankle, getting hit by a car or bitten by a loose dog are all on the forefront of the imagination, as they relate to running. While other exercise is important too, stretching, resistance training, etc., the main focus here will be on running.

Allow me to clarify something, when I say running, I am referring to everything between a 7-minute mile to a 17-minute mile. Some may say that 17 and 18-minute miles are not running, try to tell that to the 75-year-old lady that just passed the 22-mile marker in a marathon. The key point here is being out there doing something, and the speed is not that important.

Although I must add, it would be nice to get home sometime today.

This short guide is based totally on my own personal experience as a long term runner and the research I have done over the years using myself as a test subject. I truly don't know how many miles I have run since I began running in 1978. I say this because there were times when I ran a lot and other times when I didn't run too much. Keep in mind, in 1978 I was 32 years old, and the body was very resilient in those days, so 40 and 50-mile weeks were no big deal, and I did them regularly. Like everything else, things change, the body changes, motivation changes, and goals change. Most runners have visions of someday running a marathon, 26.2 miles, just to see if they can do it. The majority of runners do not take running to this level, I did. However, raising children, making a living, keeping relationships together, it all takes its toll on us and our running programs.

I used running as a way to deal with the stresses of daily life, I still do today as I get ready to turn 70 years old. Fortunately, at this stage of life, many of the former stressors of life are gone. The children have grown up and are now on their own making their way in life. Making a living is less of an issue now that pensions and social security benefits have started. Relationships are settled now, and my wife and I are coming up on 50 years of marriage, having survived the ups and downs that go along with staying together for such a long time. There is still a strong commitment to go as long as the good Lord lets us hang around. By the way, she is not a runner and thinks I'm nuts.

I understand that everyone's situation is different, but that is where running comes into the picture. Running is always the same, it something that is constant and that we can do anywhere, at any time. Regardless of the kind of day you have, a short run can make it better. If just a limited period of time, you can focus on something that you have control over. This applies at any age and can be extremely helpful as we get older.

I talk with people all the time that have already passed that 50-year milestone and truly, many have resigned themselves to the fact that they are now old and no longer able to do things that they used to, running may be one of those things. Truth be told, age can be one of those things that is a self-fulfilling prophecy, if you think you are old, then, guess what, you will probably starting acting and feeling old. I still feel at least 20 years younger than I am, and I hope to continue to stay that way as I move into my seventh decade of life.

In 2013, at age 67, I ran a 4k run here in Las Vegas, NV with about 300 other people, a small race in comparison to other races I have run. The run was a beer run. Each runner that wanted some and was old enough to have some could have an 8-ounce cup of beer at the start of the run, another in the middle of the race and more at the end. It was a great time, with music, people laughing and overall having a great experience. When it was all over, and we were all waiting for the awards ceremony, my name was called. I went up to the stage, and it was announced that I was the oldest runner that had signed up and run the race. When I was asked how come I was still running at 67, I simply answered, "Because I still can, and it keeps me young." I got a great applause, and afterward, many younger runners came up to me, shook my hand and said, "Boy I sure hope I can be like you when I get to 67." You have no idea how great that made me feel.

I truly believe that running has kept me young mentally and to a lesser degree physically. Sure I have aches and pains when I get up in the morning. Sometimes my knees ache, or my hips hurt some, but I get up, do some light stretching exercises and in a short time, I'm ready to go. Are there times when I don't want to do it, of course, but the alternative is to get stiff joints and to a point where I can't even tie my own shoes. I know people like this who are younger than I am.

In the Beginning

If you are a senior citizen and contemplating doing a little running by all means, get started. First, though, talk to your doctor and make sure it is okay for you to start a running program. Most doctors will give you a green light, providing you don't have any serious medical issues. Once you get clearance from your doctor, it is just a matter of getting started.

I will not blow smoke at you, running can be hard, particularly at the beginning. As a senior you have lived life, and you have lots of experience in many things. The experiences that you have had can be detrimental to your running program. I say this because, on those days that you don't feel like running, you will use those experiences to make up excuses not to go out and run.

Trust me; I have been down that road many times. Not long ago I was having one of those days. I was going to go out for a 3-mile run that morning, but I got up feeling a little lazy and sluggish. I had slept well, and there was really no reason for not going out to run. I putted around, making coffee, writing in my journal, and doing anything that kept me from lacing up my running shoes and getting out the door. Finally, when my wife asked me if I was going, I said, "No, not today, I have to get the oil changed in the car." I goofed around all day long and didn't do my run as I had previously planned.

That night, as I sat around watching television, I kept thinking, "I should have gone for my run this morning. It would have taken me about 45 minutes, and I could have easily done it, but I had talked myself out of it. It is easy to find excuses when you just don't want to go run and unfortunately the more life experiences you have under your belt, the more excuses you can come with when you need one. It was too late to do anything about the morning run that I missed, but the next day I was back out there again doing what I should have done the day before.

Speaking of schedules, as a senior runner, you should not attempt to run every day, particularly if you are just starting. Read any book on running and there will be some schedules and routines presented by the authors, who by the way are mostly younger runners and have little or no knowledge regarding what it means to run after 50 years old. Hard to know what an older runner feels like if you are not one yourself. Many of these books present programs that call for running lots of miles in a variety of strategies, including sprints, which can be really bad for a senior runner. They may also call for hill and speed work, which can also be detrimental to a senior runner. Unless you are in superb physical condition, I would recommend you stay away from these routines.

As a senior runner, your starting routine should be three days a week. Any schedule that allows you to go out and do something then rest the next day will allow your body to adapt to the new stress that running imposes on you. For example, a Monday, Wednesday, Friday routine, 20-30 minutes on each day is a great starting point. Do some light stretching exercises before and after your run, nothing extensive though?

These exercises should be simple: touch your toes bending over if you can, if you can't go down as far as you can and try to go a little further each day. Reach up to the sky with both hands and bend backward just a little. Put your hands on your hips and twist at the waist from side to side for a few repetitions. You are not looking to do a full blown stretching routine here, although that, come later. For right now, all you want to do is loosen up a bit before you go out and run. The same routine after your run will help relax you too. This is not rocket science, it is just physiology.

One thing I learned the hard way is that if I don't do some stretching before and after a run, I experience a higher degree of muscle soreness the following day. I don't know if this because I am older or if it there is some other reason. To avoid the issue of soreness I just do the stretches and that seems to work just fine. Try it; what do you have to lose?

Some beginning runners get all hung up on running gear. What type of shoes, which are really important by the way, shorts, shirts, watches, music devices and all kinds of other stuff. Here is what I have learned about that through trial and error, the most important thing to concentrate on is your shoes. The right pair will save your feet and legs; the wrong pair will literally hurt you.

When I began running, many decades ago, I knew nothing about running or running shoes. Hey, how hard could it be, you just get a pair of basketball sneakers and go out and run right? Wrong. There were no "running stores" in those days. People that were out running were thought to be some kind of kooks, and people looked at you like your elevator didn't go all the way up. So I went to some local chain store, I think it may have been a J.C. Penny store, went to the shoe section and saw a pair of flashy yellow sneakers. I bought the shoes with great excitement and went out to my old high school running track behind the fire station. The school had long since closed, and the track hadn't been used in years, it was overgrown with weeds, but there was still some semblance of a quarter mile loop visible. With my super flashy yellow shoes on, I took off like a shot! By the time, I hit the first turn at the end of the straightaway I was huffing and puffing and thought I was going to puke. My knees were already hurting, and I had a pain in my side rib cage.

As a typical newbie, I gave up and walked back to my car thinking, boy this was a stupid idea. I decided to do a little more research and find some runners to talk to before I tried this again. A few days later I found a guy that was a runner, about ten years younger than I was, and I showed him my shoes and told him about my track experience. He said the shoes I had were made playing badminton on grass, not for running. He gave me the names of a couple of brands and recommended I buy a pair of those shoes before I ran again. I bought a pair of the latest Nike shoes, and they worked out well.

Here is what I recommend regarding running shoes. Find a specialty running store in your area or close by and visit the store. Talk to the people working in the store and find out what they know about runners and if they have ever worked with senior runners. Most of the time these individuals are runners too, but they may be limited in their knowledge of working with older runners. The good store employees will ask you some questions: are you new to running, have you ever run before, how much do you plan to run, are you road running or trail running, these are all common questions which you should be prepared to answer. Many of these stores will have an indoor treadmill, and they will have you walk on the treadmill barefooted while either videotaping you or just observing your walking style and perhaps a slow run. The purpose of this activity is to get an idea how your foot lands on the ground and whether or not you have mechanical issues that can be mitigated by the shoes you buy. For example, do you have flat feet or high arches, does your foot roll to the inside or the outside. These are important issues that can be addressed with properly fitting shoes and prevent injury when you start to run.

Once the analysis is made, they will likely bring out a variety of shoes of different brand names and styles. You will get to try the shoes on and either walk or run in them before you buy them. The most important part of this entire process is that they fit well and that you are satisfied with your purchase when you leave the store. If you have any mechanical issues in your foot placement, the shoes you buy should correct those issues.

Some shoes are neutral for people that have a solid heel to toe footfall. Others provide stability to help correct pronation problems (your foot turning either inward or outward when it lands). Once those areas are determined you will be able to select a proper pair of shoes that will be best for you. It is important to try shoes of different brands at the same time, for example, a Nike shoe on your left foot and a New Balance shoe on your right foot. Using this approach will allow you to find the one that feels the best for your foot. It can take a little while to go through all this so make sure you have plenty of time when you go to buy your shoes. Remember, you are going to be spending a lot of time in these shoes, and you want them to be the best they can be for you.

Most store helpers will not try to "sell" you on a pair of shoes, they will do their best to find the right pair for you and ensure that you are absolutely satisfied with them before you leave the store. Do not buy something that does not feel great on your feet, because all those shoes will do for you is cause you problems. Now for the bad news, a good pair of running shoes is going to set you back about $120, when I bought my first Nike pair in 1978 I paid about $35, the last pair of Brooks shoes I bought, last year were $110. I look at it this way, if you divide the cost by the number of miles you run in a month, the cost becomes minimal.

Other items like running shirts or singlets are usually a matter of personal taste; just make sure they fit well. For most seniors a loose fitting shirt is much more comfortable than a tight fitting shirt. The same goes for running shorts in good weather. Back in the day when running first became popular, tiny shorts were the popular item and seniors looked pretty strange in those shorts. I have a few scary memories photos of those days. Today, larger, more comfortable shorts are common in warm weather. Cold weather obviously requires different clothing and most runners will layer their clothes in cold weather conditions. Layers work because initially it can be really cold, but as you get warmed up, you may need to remove some of the clothing you put on, or you will overheat.

Just some final points regarding winter running, as a senior runner your most important challenge, is to stay healthy. Winter running can be fun, but it can also be dangerous. Every year runners in cold climates slip and fall, which usually sidelines them from running. Also, because of changes in body temperatures in cold climates, seniors are subject to colds, flu, and pneumonia. If any of these are a concern, consider running indoors, either on a treadmill or other indoor location. Taking care of yourself is paramount when you are a senior.

If you have read this far it tells me that you are interested in running, and about now you are saying, "Ok, ok, I know all that, but how do I actually get started?" Very good question, so let's get to it.

Getting Started

For the sake of this description, we will assume that it is a nice day, the sun is shining, and the temperature is around 50 degrees, no wind, no rain, an ideal running day. Once you have gotten dressed in your new running outfit, whatever that may be, you have a few decisions to make as you get ready to head out the door.

Where are you going to go to start your first run? Are you just going to go around your neighborhood, or are you going to drive to park somewhere, perhaps a high school running track that is not being used. Okay, you have decided and are ready to go. Start with a brisk walk, since this is your first time, walk for 5 minutes (your watch will become your friend on these outings). At the end of the 5 minutes, stop and stretch just a little, how do you feel? A few bend over's, arms up in the air and a few squats (not very deep squats).

Now that is a good start, and you can continue on with a slow run for one minute, walk for one minute. If that feels okay, try a two-minute run and a one minute walk. For this first time, continue the process, two minutes running, one minute walking. You can try three minutes running and one-minute walking also if everything feels good. This becomes the beginning of your running journey for the first month. Using this approach will allow your muscles, tendons and ligaments to get accustomed to the additional stress you are putting on them.

(The remainder of this short book will share some of my experiences as a runner and introduce you to some of the great people I met

while on the roads or trails). As we go along we will change your run/walk time schedule, so stay with me.

During your second month, you can add another minute to the run and another minute to the walk. I know lots of seniors that use a three-minute run with a two-minute walk, and they can cover really long distances using this method, including half and full marathons. I personally have completed several half marathons using this approach in the last ten years.

A realization that we all must face is that as older athletes (and you are an athlete, don't forget that), we have limits. We cannot run as fast, we don't recover as quickly after a hard run (like a race), and the chances are good that we are not going to make the Olympic team, so take it easy. Remember you are doing this for fun and to improve your overall health, not to hurt yourself.

One of the biggest mistakes made by new runners, regardless of age or gender, is attempting to do too much too soon. It is a natural temptation, you go out and run, and you feel great so you decide, "Hey I can go out again today," and you skip your rest day. You go out and hit it hard, you have a good run. The following day your knee hurts a little, but it is a scheduled run day so you go out and limp along even though the knee is hurting. The next day, the knee hurts so bad you can hardly put any weight on it. How do I know this? Been there, done that. This is new to your body, allow yourself some adjustment time and take it slow.

Over the years I have talked with lots of beginning runners of all ages that want to quit after a couple of weeks or so of running, claiming that they were not made to be a runner. When I ask them about their running program, they tell me they are either running every day, or they are running more than 30 minutes during one session. Also, they tell me they are running fast, a recipe for disaster.

Not only will these approaches cause a new runner to quit, but they also have the potential to cause injury which can take a long time to get over. A fellow I know started his journey by running too fast on a trail. He twisted an ankle by stepping on a rock that rolled over. He was about two miles from his truck and hobbled along with a stick till he got back. By the time he got back to town, his ankle had swelled and was really hurting. He went straight to the emergency room at the hospital, and they determined that it was a very bad sprain, but it was not broken. He decided his running days were over, and he had only been running for two months. It took him about two months to get back to normal and eventually he did start running again, much slower this time and in a friendlier environment, a park. My recommendation, take your time, don't rush to run fast or to run long, that will come if that is what your goal is for your running program. If you enjoy your evolution t being an athlete and a runner, you will have a long and memorable running life.

Racing

Many senior runners want to run just to get into shape, maybe to try to lose a little weight (I'll talk about that a little later), but some want to try racing. Racing is fun and gives you a great sense of really being an athlete and being young again. Remember the days when you could just take off at a run without even giving it thought, you just did it. Those were probably the days before your twentieth birthday.

Today, depending on your age now, running is not something you normally do on the spur of the moment, barring some sort of emergency. Running races, regardless of the distance, gives you that old feeling of youth. From the moment you sign up for a race, your mind is already in gear, thinking about the details of the race.

First off, how long is it? Where is it? How will you get there? What will you wear? If it's out of town, where will you stay? (One of my greatest experiences was the half marathon at Disneyland in California; we stayed at the Disneyland Hotel and made a big weekend out of the event). All those are questions that pop up as you sign the racing application and pay your fee. As a beginning runner, if you want to race, I would recommend a 5k (3.1 miles) fun run. Your first run will be a little nerve racking because you are not sure what to expect. There are numerous 5k runs in cities all around the country, and it is not difficult to find one. Most of these runs are advertised on the internet and allow runners to register online.

Depending on the size of the event, the race fees will vary, as well as the amenities provided for the runners. Most will offer a finishers medal and/or a t-shirt. Normally there are refreshments available after the race and lots of commentaries as finishers and friends wait around for the awards ceremony. Not everyone waits around for the ceremony, but those who do often have lots of fun. I have run in 5ks with as few as 50 runners and others with thousands of runners. Some of the half marathons and marathons in larger cities can get up into the tens of thousands, and those are really an adventure worth remembering.

The atmosphere at the race is always exciting. People are milling around doing all kinds of strange things. Some are stretching, some are jogging around slowly, some are just standing around by themselves, and others are in groups. One thing is common at every race; the lines at the Porta-Potties are always long. People are nervous and need to go to the restroom. Many runners are checking their shoes, their watches, and GPS readings. Some are checking out their music if they have any.

Others are applying Vaseline or other lubricants to a variety of places on their bodies.

The time of day can also be a factor, but most races are run first thing in the morning. A few years ago I ran the Extra-terrestrial Half Marathon in Rachel, Nevada, next to Area 51. The race started at 12 midnight, in a pitch-black stretch of highway in the middle of the desert. It was a marvelous experience and one that you normally look back on and say, "Wow, I can't believe I did that." All the runners and there were about 300, were wearing headlights and neck glow sticks, and we were all bouncing up and down in the darkness. It truly looked like something out of science fiction movie.

These types of races are unique and provide most runners with lifetime memories, but even the smaller races can be fun. I have met some of the most wonderful people at these small races, and many have become friends that I still stay in touch with over the internet.

At the opposite end of that spectrum are the huge races, most of the time longer than 5k, usually half marathons (13.1 miles), although I have run some 15k runs too (9 miles), and of course the full marathons. For example, many runners love the Rock n Roll marathon series. These are usually, half and full marathons, although recently some of these are also offering what is called a half of the half, a 10k run (6.2 miles). This series tends to draw a very large crowd of runners. By large, I mean in the thousands of runners. The last one that I ran in Las Vegas, NV had over 30,000 participants. That is a big race by anyone's standards.

In the beginning, most new runners, particularly senior runners, may be intimidated by these huge races. There is nothing wrong with not jumping into these races and sticking to the smaller races. Smaller races are a good place to learn about yourself and how you react to competition. One thing that I learned is that regardless of the race, there was always someone at the end of the race that was racing against me, no matter how slow we were running. What is fun for me is that most of the time, these individuals are about half my age, sometimes they beat me and sometimes I beat them at the end. But it is all about friendly competition.

The reality is though that most likely the days of coming in with the leaders is long past; however, there is a silver lining, it's called age. Why age? Because most races are broken into age groups, all runners participate together, but the results are divided by age group and sometimes gender as well. For example, in the last five years, I have come in several times being first in my age group because there are no other competitors as old as I am. So, if you stay at it long enough, you too will get some of those first place awards after you are an oldie, but a still strong athlete.

Back to the Real World

While races are certainly fun, and many people train regularly so that they can participate in races, the majority of senior runners run regularly for their own personal reasons. There are some runners that like to run with a group, but most training is done alone, you will spend a lot of time in your own head if you decide to become a runner. Partners and group runs are not always reliable or may not always fit into your schedule. Don't discount running with a partner or a group, but be prepared to do your own thing.

Some beginning runners have difficulty with the solitude, it can be disconcerting. Most people are not used to spending so much time in their own company; this becomes more of an issue when the runs become longer. For the most part running is a solo act. There are benefits to being alone with your thoughts on a road or a trail. Many ideas are generated while out on a run, problems can be worked out and solutions found. If nothing else the run serves as a form of stress relief.

When my mother passed away many years ago, I was able to deal with the grief by running. I was getting ready for a marathon and the long runs helped by giving me time to process the loss. Over the years, I have spoken with other runners who have also used running to work through all sorts of problem situations. Being able to get inside your own head during these times can be very beneficial. Does it work every time? No. However, having something to do other than focus on the problem can yield amazing results.

If you find yourself in need of connecting to your spiritual side, there is no better way to do so then by going out for a run. When you are out on the road or trail, regardless of the time of day or weather, you have the opportunity to see all the wonders that nature provides for you every day. Smell the air, feel the heat or the cool of the day on your face, look at the sky and the trees. These are all gifts from God to you, the runner.

As you begin your run, take in the sights that are on your route. For this particular run, leave your music off, if you normally listen to music. Instead, listen to the sounds of the day. What do you hear? Birds, the wind, barking dogs, car noise, all are possible sounds you may hear.

Perhaps more importantly than those external noises is what you hear inside yourself. We all talk to ourselves, so what are you saying to yourself as you go about your run? Many times this internal voice is a divine power speaking to you, helping you work through some problem.

Extending Your Life

There is still controversy regarding whether or not running can extend life. Since I am not a scientist or professional researcher, I can only tell you what I have experienced in my own life and through observations of other older runners. At the present time, I am just about to turn 70 years old, and I run/walk 12-15 miles every week. I do have friends that already in their 70's that run 20 miles a week or more. The one's that run more have been running most of their adult lives.

I am not implying that running alone can extend your life. Obviously, a person should also lead a healthy lifestyle. A well-balanced diet of carbohydrates, fats and proteins will help fuel your muscles and your mind. Not too much fast food, taking appropriate vitamin supplements, and not indulging in excess alcohol, and by all means, no smoking of any kind.

Maintaining a healthy lifestyle also includes keeping your strength up. A great way to do this is by doing a little resistance training a couple of times a week. Some older runners belong to a gym or fitness center, and that can make it easy to do some resistance training because they usually have free weights or machines to help do the exercises. But that is not necessary; resistance training can be done at home. Exercises like pushups, squats, climbing stairs, and doing some lifting of things around your house can be beneficial. For example, fill a bucket with water and lift it over your head, you'll only spill it once, then you will make sure you get strong enough not to do that again.

The other thing that strength training will do for you is to improve your bone density. Think about the many people that you might have heard about that fall when they are older, and they break a hip or leg, and that event leaves them in a debilitated state for months. Don't be afraid that you are going to build huge muscles, that simply will not happen, but you will get stronger.

For a person who is not familiar with weight training, it is highly recommended that a professional trainer is consulted. It might cost a few dollars, but it will be worth it to learn how to lift weights or use machines properly so that you don't hurt yourself. A professional trainer will understand what you are trying to do and help you to get started. Remember, your objective is to get and stay healthy, not to build excess muscle. When you see individuals with lots of muscle mass, you should be aware that these individuals are on very strict diets and training programs to purposely obtain those results. The work required to be a body builder is extreme and not really something that the average senior should engage in.

A key activity that many times is overlooked is the simple act of walking. While running is good, so is walking, and there will be times when you feel that this is a good alternative to a run day. Here is an example, for whatever reason, you just don't feel like running today, rather than totally space off the day and the opportunity, take a walk. A walk is just that, a leisurely walk along whatever route you feel is the best for you at the time.

There are some runners, myself being one of them that have learned and practiced the art of race-walking and that works well for me as an alternative exercise when I don't feel like running, or I am recovering from some minor injury. Now race walking does not have to be at Olympic speed, it can be done slowly, easily and deliberately. There are some race walkers that can actually walk faster than some slow runners. If you have an interest in race walking, I encourage you to go to the internet and check out the various videos that are available on YouTube in the sport of race walking. Remember, you don't have to be able to do it the way they do it in the video. With practice, however, you can get pretty good at it.

Some of the advantages of walking are that it puts much less strain and your tendons and ligaments, and you rarely will experience muscle soreness. Because you are moving at a much slower pace, you can enjoy the environment around you much more than when you are running and moving quickly. Walking also will give you the opportunity to think about things, such as problems you might want to solve or ideas that you are considering.

As with running, make sure that you get a proper pair of shoes for the activity, regular sneakers bought from a chain store will probably cause you to experience foot or leg problems. You can wear your running shoes for walking with no ill effects. Unless you have some particular reason for wanting to walk a long way, consider walking for about 30-40 minutes at most. In truth there seems to be some opinion that walking beyond that length of time provides few, if any additional physical benefits.

The walk for a 30-40 minute period will help raise your heart rate and will release endorphins into your system which will help you feel better and think more clearly. Runners sometimes talk about something similar that is referred to as "runners high." I have experienced this only a few times in the many years that I have been running. A runner's high happens when you are running in what athletes refer to as "the zone." You are running without really thinking about it, and the run seems to be almost effortless. At some point in the run, you realize that you have covered a long distance without being conscience of the effort that it took to get to where you are.

Getting back to the walking issue, don't discount the many benefits that can be gained by a simple walking program. Many beginning runners of all ages find that they enjoy walking more than they do running and therefore change their program to accommodate walking days instead of running days. These types of programs can be especially good for someone that is just starting, may be dealing with some form of physical issue or someone that is initially fearful of what running might do to them.

Dealing with Injuries

It would be unrealistic to write any book that deals with fitness and senior citizens and not deal with the fact that injuries are part of the package. Hopefully, as it has been for me, the few injuries have been minor. For the most part, the injuries I have experienced have been the result of doing more than I should have been doing. Things like running too far, running for too long a period of time without taking walking breaks, running too fast and not taking enough rest days in between runs, particularly long runs. For example, if you normally run 3-mile runs during the week and then take off on a 7 miler on the weekend, you may need two rest days after that 7 milers before going out again for your regular 3-mile run. This is really important if you exceed 10 miles on a long run; take more rest time before going out again.

In my younger days, I would run almost every day, and there was little to worry about because I recovered quickly. As I got older, I realized that I needed more rest and recovery time. As time went on, I came to understand that if I didn't take the time to rest, I was going to be dealing with more muscle soreness or would risk getting injured.

At this stage of my life, I run three days a week and only 3-5 miles at a time, depending on how I feel. I weight train two days a week for about 30 minutes, and I rest completely on two other days, no exercise at all other than my morning stretches. Let me be clear about something, those 3-5 mile run days are done using the run/walk method. On a good day, when all is working well I will run 3 minutes and walk 2 minutes. I use this process until I am done with my miles for the day. On average, I will finish the run at a 15 minute per mile pace and that is just fine with me. For some, that pace is barely moving, for a 70-year-old that is a miracle.

It is important to recognize that there may be times when you will have to seek out the help of a health care professional for something that happened to you as a result of your running activities. Chiropractors, physical therapists, other general practitioners or specialty doctors may also be necessary. Don't let this scare you off, these are the exceptions rather than the rule.

Let me share an example with you. Not long ago I was experienced severe pain in the bottom of my left heel first thing in the morning when I put my foot on the floor as I was getting out of bed. I did all kinds of research over several days and concluded that I had a case of something that is known as "plantar fasciitis." This is a condition that results from running too much on hard surfaces, like concrete and asphalt. As I looked at my running log, I could clearly see that most of my recent running had been on the concrete sidewalk at one of the local parks.

The pain results from the tightening of muscle that runs from the bottom of the foot. The remedy is stretching of the calf muscle I the leg, ice on the bottom of the foot and rolling the foot over a golf ball. These are all home remedies, along with some Ibuprofen. After a few weeks, I was getting no relief, and this had essentially stopped my running program. I did go to the gym and do alternative exercise on the stationary bike and the elliptical trainer (which I hate). Finally, I decided to go see my doctor, and he essentially told me what I already knew and gave me some other exercises to do. By now the pain was subsiding and in another week, all was back to normal again.

I recalled that about 20 years ago I had had a similar bout of this same condition while training for a marathon. At that time, I had gone to the doctor, and he had given me a cortisone injection right on the bottom of the heel, and it felt like it came out the top of my head. The pain did go away in a day of so because the cortisone reduced the inflammation of that plantar muscle. So there are some drawbacks occasionally to the running game, but overall those are few and far between.

On other occasions, I have suffered from various types of knee discomfort and these have been attributed to running shoes that have already exhausted their useful running life. We all wear out shoes differently depending on a variety of factors, but on average you should be able to get about 300-500 miles out of a pair of good quality running shoes. I tend to average on the high end of that number and have had some that went even a little more.

At this point, I must issue a warning. If you do become involved in running for the long term, you will find that you collect running shoes. You want to try out new models when they come out, even if you still have a perfectly good pair. You will have drawers full of running socks, closets full of running shirts and shorts. If you are doing any distance running, you will have numerous types of water bottles on an assortment of belts. As of this writing, I have in my closet twelve different pairs of running shoes. I do try to alternate occasionally, but like many other things I have my favorites, same with shorts and shirts.

Other Resources

Just a little information on some of the other resources that are available to you as a runner and that you may wish to consider. I have been a subscriber to Runner's World and Running Times magazines for years. For quite some time I used to keep every issue but after a while I found I had boxes full of old magazines in my garage, and the chances of reading them again was highly unlikely, so I got rid of them. Today, I still keep the last twelve months of these magazines just in case. In the case of what I don't know, I just can't seem to be able to read them and then toss them out.

There are some running clubs in my community, and I have gone to some of their meetings occasionally. I found, however, that for me, running tends to be a solitary activity and I just can't get into the idea of getting up and having to meet at some designated spot to go run. I think there is a place for all this, and I admire the people that do get involved in these activities. Many times they do some get charity work by sponsoring running activities to raise money.

Perhaps of most benefit is what has recently been termed "virtual races." There are some sites online, Run For Bling, U.S. Roadrunning, and Virtual Strides, that sponsor virtual races every month. The way it works is that you sign up for a particular race, pay your race fee, which is usually very reasonable, then on your honor you run your race at a time and place of your own choosing. After you're done with your race, you can post your time on the website for the sponsor. Your race fee entitles you to a race number bib, which you normally are able to print right off of your home computer and then you will receive a nice race medal in the mail for completing your race. Again, this is all on the honor system, so don't want to cheat because you will just be cheating yourself. I have completed, 5ks, 10ks, and one-half marathon using this virtual race methodology.

If you really get into the virtual race game, you can race several times a month without ever having to leave home and deal with all the other stuff that goes along with participating in a real race. For some people that I know this has been the best motivation, they could find for continuing to run on a regular basis. Check it out and give at least one race a try, I think you will like it.

The Future

Most seniors that run tend to be very optimistic about life and the time they have left on the planet. Don't get me wrong, the aches and pains of getting older are there almost every day. Running is not going to make those aches go away, as a matter of fact on some days they may be worse, like after a race or a long run. The payoff is the psychological boost that you get just knowing you can still go out and run.

A few years ago I decided to run the Lake Tahoe Half Marathon. I did my training and felt I was ready on race day. Once the race started, I realized I had underestimated the difficulty of the task at hand. I had not considered how steep the hills were or how long some of the upgrades were along the course. Additionally, I did not think about how the high altitude would affect me. Las Vegas is about 2000 feet; Lake Tahoe is over 7000 feet. The upshot of the altitude is that there is less air available to take into your lungs at the higher altitude, so you are sucking the wind trying to breathe. I struggled throughout the entire race, especially the second half of the race. I finished in a time much longer than I had anticipated, but I finished.

That night as I lay in bed at the motel, I got a cramp in my right calf that made me cry. My calf was sore for days after the experience. It had taken several weeks before I was ready to go out and run again. Despite my experience, a few weeks later I was already considering doing a 10k (6.2 miles) race, which I did do with no ill effects. The point is, take the time to recover after a race or a long run and you will reap the benefits.

Keep in mind that recovery does not always mean going back to the days when you did absolutely no exercise. There are always methods of alternative training without running. You can still strength train, or swim, do some underwater running in a pool, which is very beneficial and don't forget simply walking.

The point is that your future will be better if your body is still able to move around and do everyday things that you have always done. Think about some of those people that turn 60 and feel, look and act as if they are already past

80. Many of these people die before their time because they give up on life and the wondrous things that are in store for them in their older years.

If you have gotten to this point, you are likely not one of those people that have to worry about getting old. You know exactly where you are and have seen the light. You are looking at ways to make improvements starting right now and for that, I congratulate you. As I close out this short book, remember, there are lots of running resources out on the market. The internet is full of encouraging information, take advantage of it, and just keep in mind that many times the information is aimed at younger runners.

Many older people are hesitant to get involved in any kind of exercise after they pass a certain age, and that age is different for everyone. Some people feel old at 45, others are still doing things at 75 or 80 that they were doing when they were 45. My father is a prime example, he is now 89, and he still goes fishing in the summer months, and seems to be constantly involved in some type of construction project around his house. He still drives everywhere even though his is required to take a driving and eye test every year. He does not seem to be slowing down much, but he does complain about arthritis in his knees.

Some people may say that it is all about having good genes and perhaps there is some validity to that idea, but it also has a lot to do with how we take care of ourselves. Barring some catastrophic illness or accident, we all have the opportunity to improve our lifestyle and situation in life. It is not easy, it does take some effort, and there will be family members that may try to discourage you.

Not long ago I was talking with a 66-year-old woman that was interested in starting a running program. She had heard some other people in the school where we teach part time that I had recently finished a 5k race, and she wanted to talk with me regarding how she could do that also. We had a nice conversation that covered many of the topics in this book, and she went home very excited about the possibility of starting a running program. The following day her enthusiasm had totally dissipated, and I asked her what happened. She explained that she had talked with her 45-year-old daughter about the idea, and her daughter had convinced her that all she would be doing would be setting her up for more health problems. With the best of intentions, her daughter had doomed her to a life of an old person, minimizing her active lifestyle.

If you want to start a running program, don't let anyone talk you out of it because there will be many that will try. One of the problems in our society is that young people many times think they know what is best for their older family members. They forget that most of us have lived a long life already and have a history of experience doing things we had never done before and running is no exception.

Old age is a matter of attitude unless of course you do have serious physical issues to contend with, in which case you just need to do the best you can. But, don't let your previous ideas about what it means to be old impact your future. If you are reading this book, it tells me that you are not buying into all that stuff about not being able to be active when you are moving on in years. Look around you, there are all types of people, of all ages, doing all types of activities that make them happy. You are able to do whatever you set your mind to doing, it is just a matter of being careful and doing things in moderation.

Having said to be moderate, I have to walk that back a bit because not to long ago I met an old guy at a race that put that idea on the back burner. I say, old guy because he was 76 years old. As we stood there talking before the race started, I asked him if he had been running long. He said that he had been running for about 30 years and had run dozens of full marathons, and now he had moved on. I was puzzled, I asked, "Moved on to what?" I am now doing ultra-marathons he said, with a grin on his face. He went on to say that in his opinion, ultra-marathons were actually easier for him because they were more about mental toughness than physical abilities.

"There is lots of walking in an ultra-marathon," he said. Speed is not something that you hear or read about in most publications that talk about ultra-running. You might be curious regarding what constitutes an ultra-marathon. An ultra-marathon is anything beyond the traditional 26.2-mile marathon distance. The most popular ultras are 100k (62 miles) and 100m (100 miles). Sounds unbelievable, but the sport is growing more popular every year, and many of the people doing these are senior participants.

So there you have it, a long list of possibilities for you to consider as you embark upon you running journey. I am continuing my journey too by doing what I enjoy most, and that is being out there, regardless of the time or distance.

I wish you the best in your quest for better health and happy running.

Made in the USA
Lexington, KY
12 December 2018